IF FOUND PLEASE KINDLY RETURN TO:

NAME:

_____

CELL:

_____

THE ENNEAGRAM PRAYER JOURNAL

Created to remind
you of God's Goodness
in every season.

Published by Journal Hub
Los Angeles, California

Copyright © My Prayer Journal 2019

Scripture quotations marked (NIV) are taken from the THE HOLY BIBLE, NEW INTERNATIONAL VERSION®, NIV® Copyright © 1973, 1978, 1984, 2011 by Biblica, Inc.™ Used by permission. All rights reserved worldwide.

If you are interested in bulk orders for your church or organization, message us at enneagramjournal.co/contact

Lets get Personal.

Who does this journal belong to?
_____

What does your relationship with Jesus look like?
_____

How often do you pray?
_____

City & State you live in?
_____

Do you currently attend a church? If so, what do you love about it?
_____

Group of friends that you will journal with to keep accountable to:
_____

WHAT IS THE ENNEAGRAM?

The Enneagram is a personality typing system that consists of nine different types. Everyone is considered to be one single type, although one can have traits belonging to other ones.

While it's uncertain whether this type is genetically determined, many believe it is already in place at birth.

The nine types (or "enneatypes", "ennea" means "nine") are universally identified by the numbers 1 to 9.

These numbers have a standard way of being placed around the Enneagram symbol. Enneagram authors have attached their own individual names to these numbers they are as follows:

1. The Reformer
2. The Helper
3. The Achiever
4. The Individualist
5. The Investigator
6. The Loyalist
7. The Enthusiast
8. The Challenger
9. The Peacemaker

Which are you? >>

People of a particular type have several characteristics in common, but they can be quite different nevertheless.

>>

WINGS

Usually one has characteristics of one of the types that lie adjacent to one's own that are more prominent. This is called the wing. So someone who is a type 5, might have a 4 wing or a 6 wing. This may be abbreviated to "5w4" and "5w6". If one doesn't have a dominant wing, it is said that the wings are balanced

Type 1

Perfectionists, responsible, fixated on improvement

Ones are essentially looking to make things better, as they think nothing is ever quite good enough. This makes them perfectionists who want to reform and improve, who desire to make order out of the omnipresent chaos.

Type 2

Helpers who need to be needed.

Twos essentially feel that they are worthy insofar as they are helpful to others. Love is their highest ideal. Selflessness is their duty.

Giving to others is their reason for being.

Involved, socially aware, usually extroverted, Twos are the type of people who remember everyone's birthday and who go the extra mile to help out a co-worker, spouse or friend in need.

Type 3

Focused on the presentation of success, to attain validation.

Threes need to be validated in order to feel worthy; they pursue success and want to be admired. They are frequently hard working, competetive and are highly focused in the pursuit of their goals, whether their goal is to be the most successful salesman in the company or the "sexiest" woman in their social circle.

Type 4

Identity seekers, who feel unique and different.

Fours build their identities around their perception of themselves as being somehow different or unique; they are thus self-consciously individualistic. They tend to see their difference from others as being both a gift and a curse - a gift, because it sets them apart from those they perceive as being somehow "common," and a curse, as it so often seems to separate them from the simpler forms of happiness that others so readily seem to enjoy.

Type 5

Thinkers who tend to withdraw and observe.

Fives essentially fear that they don't have enough inner strength to face life, so they tend to withdraw, to retreat into the safety and security of the mind where they can mentally prepare for their emergence into the world. Fives feel comfortable and at home in the realm of thought. They are generally intelligent, well read and thoughtful and they frequently become experts in the areas that capture their interest.

Type 6

Conflicted between trust and distrust.

Sixes essentially feel insecure, as though there is nothing quite steady enough to hold onto. At the core of the type Six personality is a kind of fear or anxiety. Sixes don't trust easily; they are often ambivalent about others, until the person has absolutely proven herself, at which point they are likely to respond with steadfast loyalty.

Type 7

Pleasure seekers and planners, in search of distraction.

Sevens are essentially concerned that their lives be an exciting adventure. They are future oriented, restless people who are generally convinced that something better is just around the corner. They are quick thinkers who have a great deal of energy and who make lots of plans. They tend to be extroverted, multi-talented, creative and open minded.

Type 8

Taking charge, because they don't want to be controlled.

Eights are essentially unwilling to be controlled, either by others or by their circumstances; they fully intend to be masters of their fate. Eights are strong willed, decisive, practical, tough minded and energetic.

They also tend to be domineering; their unwillingness to be controlled by others frequently manifests in the need to control others instead.

Type 9

Keeping peace and harmony.

Nines essentially feel a need for peace and harmony. They tend to avoid conflict at all costs, whether it be internal or interpersonal. As the potential for conflict in life is virtually ubiquitous, the Nine's desire to avoid it generally results in some degree of withdrawal from life, and many Nines are, in fact, introverted. Other Nines lead more active, social lives, but nevertheless remain to some to degree "checked out," or not fully involved, as if to insulate themselves from threats to their peace of mind.

Now that you have learned the Enneagram types.

Let us introduce you to your customized prayer journal >>

In the journaling pages we have pulled a verse and study questions for you to meditate on each morning. Each verse has been curated to envoke and stir reflection to your specific Ennaegram type.

Read and Respond on the lines,
Enjoy the Journey >>

Philippians 4:13

I can do all things through him who strengthens me.

Isaiah 41:10

Fear not, for I am with you; be not dismayed, for I am your God; I will strengthen you, I will help you, I will uphold you with my righteous right hand.

Deuteronomy 31:6

Be strong and courageous. Do not fear or be in dread of them, for it is the Lord your God who goes with you. He will not leave you or forsake you.

Isaiah 40:31

But they who wait for the Lord shall renew their strength; they shall mount up with wings like eagles; they shall run and not be weary; they shall walk and not faint.

1 Corinthians 10:13

No temptation has overtaken you that is not common to man. God is faithful, & He will not let you be tempted beyond your ability, but with the temptation he will also provide the way of escape, that you may be able to endure it.

Exodus 15:2

The Lord is my strength and my song, and he has become my salvation; this is my God, and I will praise him, my father's God, and I will exalt him.

Ephesians 6:10

Finally, be strong in the Lord and in the strength of his might.

Deuteronomy 20:4

For the Lord your God is he who goes with you to fight for you against your enemies, to give you the victory.

2 Corinthians 12:9-10

But he said to me, "My grace is sufficient for you, for my power is made perfect in weakness." Therefore I will boast all the more gladly of my weaknesses, so that the power of Christ may rest upon me. For the sake of Christ, then, I am content with weaknesses, insults, hardships, persecutions, and calamities. For when I am weak, then I am strong.

Joshua 1:9

Have I not commanded you? Be strong & courageous. Do not be frightened, and do not be dismayed, for the Lord your God is with you wherever you go.

2 Timothy 1:7

For God gave us a spirit not of fear but of power and love and self-control.

Isaiah 12:2

Behold, God is my salvation; I will trust, and will not be afraid; for the Lord God is my strength and my song, and he has become my salvation.

Matthew 11:28

Come to me, all who labor and are heavy laden, and I will give you rest.

Isaiah 40:29

He gives power to the faint, and to him who has no might he increases strength.

Psalm 27:1

Of David. The Lord is my light and my salvation; whom shall I fear? The Lord is the stronghold of my life; of whom shall I be afraid?

Psalm 31:24

Be strong, and let your heart take courage, all you who wait for the Lord!

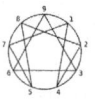

Psalm 73:26

My flesh and my heart may fail, but God is the strength of my heart and my portion forever.

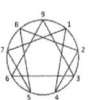

2 Corinthians 12:9

But he said to me, "My grace is sufficient for you, for my power is made perfect in weakness." Therefore I will boast all the more gladly of my weaknesses, so that the power of Christ may rest upon me.

Mark 12:30

And you shall love the Lord your God with all your heart and with all your soul and with all your mind and with all your strength.

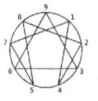

Nehemiah 8:10

Then he said to them, "Go your way. Eat the fat and drink sweet wine and send portions to anyone who has nothing ready, for this day is holy to our Lord. And do not be grieved, for the joy of the Lord is your strength."

Psalm 46:1

To the choirmaster. Of the Sons of Korah. According to Alamoth. A Song. God is our refuge and strength, a very present help in trouble.

Habakkuk 3:19

God, the Lord, is my strength; he makes my feet like the deer's; he makes me tread on my high places. To the choirmaster: with stringed instruments.

Psalm 29:11

May the Lord give strength to his people! May the Lord bless his people with peace!

John 16:33

I have said these things to you, that in me you may have peace. In the world you will have tribulation. But take heart; I have overcome the world.

1 Peter 4:11

Whoever speaks, as one who speaks oracles of God; whoever serves, as one who serves by the strength that God supplies—in order that in everything God may be glorified through Jesus Christ. To him belong glory & dominion forever and ever. Amen.

Matthew 6:33

But seek first the kingdom of God and his righteousness, and all these things will be added to you.

Psalm 23:4

Even though I walk through the valley of the shadow of death, I will fear no evil, for you are with me; your rod and your staff, they comfort me.

2 Timothy 4:17

But the Lord stood by me and strengthened me, so that through me the message might be fully proclaimed and all the Gentiles might hear it. So I was rescued from the lion's mouth.

Psalm 118:14

The Lord is my strength and my song; he has become my salvation.

2 Thessalonians 3:3

But the Lord is faithful. He will establish you and guard you against the evil one.

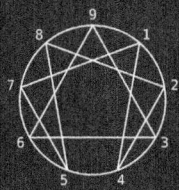

PRAYERS ANSWERED

CONGRATULATIONS YOU MADE IT THROUGH THE 30 DAYS.

PLEASE SHARE YOUR JOURNEY WITH US.

enneagramjournal.co

Printed in Great Britain
by Amazon